TensorFlow: A Complete Guide

A Step-by-Step Approach to Deep Learning, NLP, and Reinforcement Learning

Introduction to TensorFlow

What is TensorFlow? Why Use It?

TensorFlow is an open-source machine learning framework developed by Google Brain. It provides a comprehensive, flexible ecosystem for building, training, and deploying machine learning (ML) and deep learning models. Initially released in 2015, TensorFlow has evolved significantly, with version 2.x offering a more user-friendly and intuitive interface compared to its predecessor.

TensorFlow is widely used across various domains, including computer vision, natural language processing (NLP), reinforcement learning, and scientific computing. It powers applications ranging from recommendation systems and medical image analysis to autonomous vehicles and large-scale language models.

Some key reasons why TensorFlow is a popular choice among researchers and developers include:

- **Scalability:** TensorFlow supports training and deployment on CPUs, GPUs, and TPUs, making it suitable for both small-scale experiments and large-scale production systems.

- **Flexibility:** With APIs for Python, JavaScript, and C++, TensorFlow caters to a diverse set of use cases.
- **Ease of Use:** TensorFlow 2.x simplifies model building with Keras, eager execution, and intuitive debugging features.
- **Robust Ecosystem:** TensorFlow offers various tools, such as TensorFlow Lite for mobile devices, TensorFlow.js for web applications, and TensorFlow Extended (TFX) for production pipelines.

Installing TensorFlow (CPU/GPU Versions)

Before diving into TensorFlow, you need to install it on your system. The installation process varies depending on whether you want to run TensorFlow on a CPU or take advantage of a GPU for accelerated computations.

Installing TensorFlow (CPU Version)

The CPU version of TensorFlow is easier to install and works on most machines. You can install it using pip:

```bash
pip install tensorflow
```

Installing TensorFlow (GPU Version)

If you have an NVIDIA GPU and want to leverage its computational power, you'll need to install TensorFlow with GPU support. This requires:

- **NVIDIA GPU (with CUDA Compute Capability 3.5 or higher)**
- **CUDA Toolkit (compatible version for TensorFlow)**

- **cuDNN (CUDA Deep Neural Network library)**
- **NVIDIA drivers**

Once the dependencies are installed, you can install TensorFlow with GPU support using:

bash

```
pip install tensorflow-gpu
```

You can verify your installation by running:

python

```
import tensorflow as tf
print(tf.__version__)
print("GPU Available:",
tf.config.list_physical_devices('GPU'))
```

Understanding Tensors and Computational Graphs

At its core, TensorFlow operates with **tensors**, which are multi-dimensional arrays similar to NumPy arrays. Tensors serve as the primary data structure in TensorFlow and are used to represent inputs, outputs, and intermediate computations.

Example: Creating Tensors in TensorFlow

python

```
import tensorflow as tf

# Scalar (0D tensor)
scalar = tf.constant(5)

# Vector (1D tensor)
vector = tf.constant([1, 2, 3])

# Matrix (2D tensor)
matrix = tf.constant([[1, 2], [3, 4]])
```

3

```
# 3D Tensor
tensor_3d = tf.constant([[[1, 2], [3, 4]], [[5, 6],
[7, 8]]])

print(scalar, vector, matrix, tensor_3d)
```

TensorFlow also builds **computational graphs**, which define how operations on tensors are executed. These graphs allow for efficient computation by optimizing the execution order and distributing workloads across available hardware.

TensorFlow 2.x vs. 1.x: Key Differences

TensorFlow 2.x introduced several improvements over TensorFlow 1.x, making it more user-friendly and efficient. Some key differences include:

- **Eager Execution Enabled by Default:** In TensorFlow 2.x, operations are executed immediately, rather than building a static computation graph first.
- **Keras as the Standard API:** tf.keras is now the primary API for model building, replacing the complex session-based approach in TensorFlow 1.x.
- **Simplified APIs:** Many redundant functions and modules from TensorFlow 1.x have been deprecated, reducing complexity.

For those transitioning from TensorFlow 1.x, understanding these differences is crucial for writing modern, efficient deep-learning code.

Hands-on Exercise: Basic Tensor Operations

Let's perform some basic tensor operations to get familiar with TensorFlow's functionality.

```python
import tensorflow as tf

# Define two tensors
a = tf.constant([[1, 2], [3, 4]], dtype=tf.float32)
b = tf.constant([[5, 6], [7, 8]], dtype=tf.float32)

# Basic mathematical operations
sum_result = tf.add(a, b)   # Element-wise addition
product_result = tf.multiply(a, b)   # Element-wise
multiplication
dot_product = tf.matmul(a, b)   # Matrix
multiplication

print("Sum:\n", sum_result.numpy())
print("Element-wise Product:\n",
product_result.numpy())
print("Matrix Multiplication:\n",
dot_product.numpy())
```

Conclusion

This introduction has provided a high-level overview of
TensorFlow, its installation, and fundamental concepts like tensors
and computational graphs. In the upcoming chapters, we will delve
deeper into TensorFlow's core capabilities, covering neural
networks, deep learning techniques, and real-world applications.
Whether you are a beginner or an experienced developer, this
guide will help you master TensorFlow step by step.

2. Deep Learning Basics with TensorFlow

Deep learning is a subset of machine learning that focuses on neural networks with multiple layers. It has revolutionized fields such as computer vision, natural language processing, and reinforcement learning. TensorFlow, with its `tf.keras` module, simplifies the process of building and training deep neural networks.

In this chapter, we'll explore:

- The fundamentals of neural networks
- How to use `tf.keras` to build models
- Splitting data into training, validation, and test sets
- The role of activation functions and loss functions
- A hands-on exercise: Training a simple neural network

Neural Network Fundamentals

A neural network consists of layers of neurons (also called nodes) that process information. The basic structure includes:

- **Input Layer**: Accepts raw data (e.g., images, text, numbers).
- **Hidden Layers**: Perform feature extraction and transformations.
- **Output Layer**: Produces the final prediction or classification.

Each neuron in a layer connects to neurons in the next layer, passing information forward through weighted connections. The network "learns" by adjusting these weights using backpropagation and gradient descent.

Using tf.keras to Build Models

TensorFlow provides tf.keras, a high-level API for defining and training neural networks. It follows a sequential model approach, which is ideal for building simple feedforward networks.

Example: Creating a Simple Neural Network

```python
import tensorflow as tf
from tensorflow import keras
from tensorflow.keras import layers

# Define a simple feedforward neural network
model = keras.Sequential([
    layers.Dense(64, activation='relu',
input_shape=(10,)),   # Hidden layer
    layers.Dense(32, activation='relu'),   # Another
hidden layer
    layers.Dense(1, activation='sigmoid')   # Output
layer (for binary classification)
])

# Compile the model
model.compile(optimizer='adam',
loss='binary_crossentropy', metrics=['accuracy'])

# Summary of the model
model.summary()
```

This model has:

- An **input layer** that expects 10 features.
- Two **hidden layers** with 64 and 32 neurons using the ReLU activation function.
- An **output layer** with a single neuron using the sigmoid activation function (for binary classification).

Training, Validation, and Test Sets

When training a model, the dataset is typically split into three parts:

- **Training Set**: Used to train the model.
- **Validation Set**: Used to tune hyperparameters and check for overfitting.
- **Test Set**: Used to evaluate model performance on unseen data.

TensorFlow's `train_test_split` from `sklearn.model_selection` or `tf.keras.utils.split_dataset` can help create these splits.

```python
python

from sklearn.model_selection import train_test_split
import numpy as np

# Generate random data
X = np.random.rand(1000, 10)
y = np.random.randint(0, 2, 1000)

# Split into training (80%) and validation (20%) sets
X_train, X_val, y_train, y_val = train_test_split(X, y, test_size=0.2, random_state=42)
```

Understanding Activation Functions and Loss Functions

Activation Functions

Activation functions introduce non-linearity into the network, allowing it to learn complex patterns. Some commonly used activation functions include:

- **ReLU (Rectified Linear Unit)**: `max(0, x)` – Helps networks learn efficiently.
- **Sigmoid**: Outputs values between 0 and 1, suitable for binary classification.
- **Softmax**: Converts logits into probabilities for multi-class classification.

Example usage:

```python
layers.Dense(64, activation='relu')
```

Loss Functions

Loss functions measure how well a model is performing. The choice depends on the task:

- **Binary Cross-Entropy (`binary_crossentropy`)** – For binary classification.
- **Categorical Cross-Entropy (`categorical_crossentropy`)** – For multi-class classification.
- **Mean Squared Error (`mse`)** – For regression tasks.

Example usage:

```python
model.compile(optimizer='adam',
loss='binary_crossentropy', metrics=['accuracy'])
```

Step-by-Step Exercise: Training a Simple Neural Network

Now, let's train a simple model using a synthetic dataset.

```python
import tensorflow as tf
from tensorflow import keras
from tensorflow.keras import layers
from sklearn.model_selection import train_test_split
import numpy as np

# Generate synthetic data
X = np.random.rand(1000, 10)
y = np.random.randint(0, 2, 1000)

# Split data
X_train, X_val, y_train, y_val = train_test_split(X,
y, test_size=0.2, random_state=42)

# Define the model
model = keras.Sequential([
    layers.Dense(32, activation='relu',
input_shape=(10,)),
    layers.Dense(16, activation='relu'),
    layers.Dense(1, activation='sigmoid')  # Binary
classification
])

# Compile the model
model.compile(optimizer='adam',
loss='binary_crossentropy', metrics=['accuracy'])

# Train the model
```

```
history = model.fit(X_train, y_train, epochs=10,
validation_data=(X_val, y_val), batch_size=32)

# Evaluate the model
loss, accuracy = model.evaluate(X_val, y_val)
print(f"Validation Accuracy: {accuracy:.4f}")
```

Explanation of the Code

1. We generate **synthetic data** with 10 features and a binary target variable.
2. We split the data into **training and validation sets** (80% training, 20% validation).
3. We define a **sequential neural network** with two hidden layers.
4. We use **ReLU activation functions** for hidden layers and a **sigmoid activation function** for the output.
5. We **compile the model** with the Adam optimizer and binary cross-entropy loss function.
6. We train the model for **10 epochs**, using the validation data to monitor progress.
7. Finally, we **evaluate the model** and print the validation accuracy.

Conclusion

This chapter covered the basics of deep learning with TensorFlow, including:

✓ The fundamentals of neural networks

✓ How to build models using `tf.keras`

✓ The importance of training, validation, and test sets

✓ Activation functions and loss functions

✓ A hands-on exercise for training a simple neural network

3. Computer Vision with TensorFlow

Computer vision is one of the most impactful applications of deep learning, enabling machines to interpret and understand images and videos. TensorFlow provides a powerful set of tools for building and deploying computer vision models.

In this chapter, we will cover:
✅ Working with image datasets in TensorFlow
✅ Understanding and building Convolutional Neural Networks (CNNs)
✅ Transfer learning with pre-trained models
✅ Object detection and segmentation
✅ Hands-on project: Building an image classifier

Working with Image Datasets in TensorFlow

Using TensorFlow Datasets (`tfds`)

TensorFlow Datasets (`tfds`) provides ready-to-use datasets for machine learning, including popular image datasets like CIFAR-10 and ImageNet.

Example: Loading the CIFAR-10 dataset

```python
python

import tensorflow as tf
import tensorflow_datasets as tfds
```

```python
# Load dataset
dataset, info = tfds.load('cifar10',
as_supervised=True, with_info=True)

# Split dataset
train_dataset, test_dataset = dataset['train'],
dataset['test']

# Normalize images
def normalize(image, label):
    image = tf.cast(image, tf.float32) / 255.0
    return image, label

train_dataset =
train_dataset.map(normalize).batch(32)
test_dataset = test_dataset.map(normalize).batch(32)

# Check dataset info
print(info)
```

Using TFRecords for Efficient Storage

TFRecords is a format optimized for storing large datasets efficiently.

Example: Writing and reading TFRecords

python

```python
# Writing to TFRecord
with tf.io.TFRecordWriter('dataset.tfrecord') as
writer:
    for image, label in train_dataset:
        tf_example =
tf.train.Example(features=tf.train.Features(feature={
            'image':
tf.train.Feature(bytes_list=tf.train.BytesList(value=
[tf.io.encode_jpeg(image).numpy()])),
            'label':
tf.train.Feature(int64_list=tf.train.Int64List(value=
[label.numpy()]))
```

```
        }))
        writer.write(tf_example.SerializeToString())

# Reading from TFRecord
raw_dataset =
tf.data.TFRecordDataset('dataset.tfrecord')
```

Convolutional Neural Networks (CNNs) Explained

CNNs are the backbone of modern computer vision. They use **convolutional layers** to extract hierarchical features from images. The key components of a CNN include:

- **Convolutional Layers**: Apply filters to extract patterns.
- **Pooling Layers**: Reduce spatial dimensions and retain important information.
- **Fully Connected Layers**: Convert feature maps into final predictions.

Building a CNN with TensorFlow

```python
from tensorflow.keras import layers, models

# Define CNN model
model = models.Sequential([
    layers.Conv2D(32, (3, 3), activation='relu',
input_shape=(32, 32, 3)),
    layers.MaxPooling2D((2, 2)),
    layers.Conv2D(64, (3, 3), activation='relu'),
    layers.MaxPooling2D((2, 2)),
    layers.Conv2D(128, (3, 3), activation='relu'),
    layers.Flatten(),
    layers.Dense(128, activation='relu'),
    layers.Dense(10, activation='softmax')  # 10
classes for CIFAR-10
```

```
])

# Compile model
model.compile(optimizer='adam',
loss='sparse_categorical_crossentropy',
metrics=['accuracy'])

# Train model
model.fit(train_dataset, epochs=10,
validation_data=test_dataset)
```

Transfer Learning with Pre-Trained Models

Instead of training a model from scratch, we can use **pre-trained models** like MobileNet and ResNet to achieve high accuracy with minimal data.

Using MobileNet for Transfer Learning

```python
from tensorflow.keras.applications import MobileNetV2
from tensorflow.keras.models import Model
from tensorflow.keras.layers import Dense, Flatten

# Load pre-trained MobileNetV2
base_model = MobileNetV2(weights='imagenet',
include_top=False, input_shape=(224, 224, 3))

# Freeze layers
for layer in base_model.layers:
    layer.trainable = False

# Add custom layers
x = Flatten()(base_model.output)
x = Dense(128, activation='relu')(x)
output = Dense(10, activation='softmax')(x)   # Adjust
for number of classes
```

```
# Create model
model = Model(inputs=base_model.input,
outputs=output)

# Compile model
model.compile(optimizer='adam',
loss='categorical_crossentropy',
metrics=['accuracy'])
```

Object Detection and Segmentation

Object Detection with YOLO

YOLO (You Only Look Once) is a real-time object detection model. TensorFlow provides the `tf_models` repository for implementing YOLO.

```python
# Install TensorFlow Model Garden
!pip install tf-models-official

# Load pre-trained YOLO model
from official.vision.beta.tasks import yolo
model = yolo.YOLOV4()  # Example: Load YOLOv4 model
```

Semantic Segmentation with Mask R-CNN

Mask R-CNN is used for **instance segmentation**, where each object is classified and segmented separately.

```python
import tensorflow_hub as hub

# Load pre-trained Mask R-CNN
```

```
model =
hub.load("https://tfhub.dev/google/faster_rcnn/openim
ages_v4/inception_resnet_v2/1")

# Perform object detection
image_tensor =
tf.image.decode_jpeg(tf.io.read_file('image.jpg'))
detections = model(image_tensor)
print(detections)
```

Project: Build an Image Classifier with TensorFlow

Let's apply what we've learned by building an image classifier for a **custom dataset**.

1. Load and Preprocess Data

```python
import tensorflow as tf
from tensorflow.keras.preprocessing.image import
ImageDataGenerator

# Data Augmentation
datagen = ImageDataGenerator(rescale=1./255,
rotation_range=20, horizontal_flip=True,
validation_split=0.2)

# Load dataset
train_data = datagen.flow_from_directory('dataset/',
target_size=(128, 128), batch_size=32,
subset='training')
val_data = datagen.flow_from_directory('dataset/',
target_size=(128, 128), batch_size=32,
subset='validation')
```

2. Build the Model

```python

from tensorflow.keras import layers, models

model = models.Sequential([
    layers.Conv2D(32, (3, 3), activation='relu',
input_shape=(128, 128, 3)),
    layers.MaxPooling2D((2, 2)),
    layers.Conv2D(64, (3, 3), activation='relu'),
    layers.MaxPooling2D((2, 2)),
    layers.Flatten(),
    layers.Dense(128, activation='relu'),
    layers.Dense(3, activation='softmax')  # Assume 3
classes
])

# Compile model
model.compile(optimizer='adam',
loss='categorical_crossentropy',
metrics=['accuracy'])

# Train model
model.fit(train_data, validation_data=val_data,
epochs=10)
```

3. Evaluate and Save the Model

```python

# Evaluate model
loss, accuracy = model.evaluate(val_data)
print(f"Validation Accuracy: {accuracy:.4f}")

# Save model
model.save("image_classifier.h5")
```

Conclusion

In this chapter, we covered:
✓ Loading and preprocessing image datasets (TFDS, TFRecords)

✓ Understanding and building CNNs from scratch

✓ Using transfer learning with pre-trained models like MobileNet and ResNet

✓ Object detection and segmentation using YOLO and Mask R-CNN

✓ A hands-on project: Building an image classifier

4. Natural Language Processing (NLP) with TensorFlow

Natural Language Processing (NLP) is a critical area of deep learning that enables machines to understand and generate human language. TensorFlow provides powerful tools to handle text preprocessing, embeddings, sequence models, and transformers.

In this chapter, we will cover:
✅ Text preprocessing with TensorFlow and Keras
✅ Word embeddings (Word2Vec, FastText, BERT)
✅ Recurrent Neural Networks (RNNs), LSTMs, and GRUs
✅ Transformers and Attention Mechanisms
✅ Hands-on project: Sentiment analysis and text classification

---

Text Preprocessing with TensorFlow and Keras

Before feeding text into deep learning models, we must preprocess it. This includes tokenization, padding, and converting text into numerical representations.

Tokenization and Sequence Padding

Keras provides the `Tokenizer` class to convert text into sequences.

```python
```

```python
from tensorflow.keras.preprocessing.text import
Tokenizer
from tensorflow.keras.preprocessing.sequence import
pad_sequences

# Sample dataset
sentences = [
    "TensorFlow makes NLP easy",
    "Word embeddings are powerful",
    "Recurrent networks process sequences"
]

# Tokenization
tokenizer = Tokenizer(num_words=100,
oov_token="<OOV>")
tokenizer.fit_on_texts(sentences)
word_index = tokenizer.word_index

# Convert text to sequences
sequences = tokenizer.texts_to_sequences(sentences)

# Pad sequences
padded_sequences = pad_sequences(sequences,
maxlen=10, padding='post')

print("Word Index:", word_index)
print("Padded Sequences:\n", padded_sequences)
```

Text Vectorization with `TextVectorization` Layer

TensorFlow also provides a `TextVectorization` layer for handling text preprocessing.

```python
python

import tensorflow as tf

# Define text vectorization layer
vectorizer =
tf.keras.layers.TextVectorization(max_tokens=100,
output_mode='int', output_sequence_length=10)
```

```python
# Adapt vectorizer to dataset
vectorizer.adapt(sentences)

# Convert text to tensors
vectorized_text = vectorizer(sentences)
print(vectorized_text.numpy())
```

Word Embeddings: Word2Vec, FastText, and BERT

Word embeddings convert words into dense vector representations, capturing semantic meanings.

Using Pre-Trained Embeddings (Word2Vec, FastText)

TensorFlow allows us to use pre-trained embeddings like **GloVe** or **Word2Vec**.

```python
python

import numpy as np

# Load GloVe embeddings
embedding_index = {}
with open("glove.6B.100d.txt", encoding="utf-8") as f:
    for line in f:
        values = line.split()
        word = values[0]
        vector = np.array(values[1:],
dtype="float32")
        embedding_index[word] = vector

# Create an embedding matrix
embedding_dim = 100
word_index = tokenizer.word_index
embedding_matrix = np.zeros((len(word_index) + 1,
embedding_dim))
for word, i in word_index.items():
```

```python
    if word in embedding_index:
        embedding_matrix[i] = embedding_index[word]

# Define embedding layer
embedding_layer =
tf.keras.layers.Embedding(input_dim=len(word_index)+1
, output_dim=embedding_dim,
weights=[embedding_matrix], trainable=False)
```

Fine-Tuning with BERT

BERT (Bidirectional Encoder Representations from Transformers) is a powerful language model.

```python
python

import tensorflow_hub as hub
import tensorflow_text as text

# Load pre-trained BERT model
bert_preprocessor =
hub.KerasLayer("https://tfhub.dev/tensorflow/bert_en_
uncased_preprocess/3")
bert_encoder =
hub.KerasLayer("https://tfhub.dev/tensorflow/bert_en_
uncased_L-12_H-768_A-12/3")

def build_bert_model():
    text_input = tf.keras.layers.Input(shape=(),
dtype=tf.string)
    preprocessed_text = bert_preprocessor(text_input)
    outputs = bert_encoder(preprocessed_text)
    dense = tf.keras.layers.Dense(256,
activation='relu')(outputs['pooled_output'])
    output = tf.keras.layers.Dense(1,
activation='sigmoid')(dense)

    model = tf.keras.Model(inputs=text_input,
outputs=output)
    return model

bert_model = build_bert_model()
```

```
bert_model.compile(optimizer='adam',
loss='binary_crossentropy', metrics=['accuracy'])
```

Recurrent Neural Networks (RNNs), LSTMs, and GRUs

RNNs are designed to process sequential data, making them well-suited for NLP tasks.

Building an LSTM Model for Text Classification

```python
from tensorflow.keras.models import Sequential
from tensorflow.keras.layers import Embedding, LSTM, Dense

# Define LSTM model
model = Sequential([
    Embedding(input_dim=5000, output_dim=128, input_length=100),
    LSTM(128, return_sequences=True),
    LSTM(64),
    Dense(32, activation='relu'),
    Dense(1, activation='sigmoid')
])

# Compile model
model.compile(optimizer='adam',
loss='binary_crossentropy', metrics=['accuracy'])
model.summary()
```

Transformers and Attention Mechanisms

Transformers have revolutionized NLP by improving model performance on text-based tasks.

Understanding the Attention Mechanism

Attention allows the model to focus on important words in a sequence.

Example: Self-Attention Layer

python

```python
class SelfAttention(tf.keras.layers.Layer):
    def __init__(self, units):
        super(SelfAttention, self).__init__()
        self.W = tf.keras.layers.Dense(units)
        self.V = tf.keras.layers.Dense(1)

    def call(self, inputs):
        score = self.V(tf.nn.tanh(self.W(inputs)))
        attention_weights = tf.nn.softmax(score,
axis=1)
        context_vector = attention_weights * inputs
        return tf.reduce_sum(context_vector, axis=1)
```

Using a Pre-Trained Transformer Model (BERT)

python

```python
import transformers
from transformers import TFBertModel

bert_model = TFBertModel.from_pretrained("bert-base-
uncased")

# Define transformer-based model
input_word_ids = tf.keras.layers.Input(shape=(128,),
dtype=tf.int32, name="input_word_ids")
embedding = bert_model(input_word_ids)[0]
output = tf.keras.layers.Dense(1,
activation='sigmoid')(embedding[:, 0, :])

transformer_model =
tf.keras.Model(inputs=input_word_ids, outputs=output)
```

```python
transformer_model.compile(optimizer='adam',
loss='binary_crossentropy', metrics=['accuracy'])
```

Sentiment Analysis and Text Classification Project

Let's build a **sentiment analysis model** using TensorFlow.

1. Load and Preprocess Data

python

```python
import tensorflow_datasets as tfds

# Load IMDB dataset
dataset, info = tfds.load("imdb_reviews",
as_supervised=True, with_info=True)
train_data, test_data = dataset["train"],
dataset["test"]

# Preprocess data
train_data =
train_data.batch(32).prefetch(tf.data.AUTOTUNE)
test_data =
test_data.batch(32).prefetch(tf.data.AUTOTUNE)
```

2. Build the Model

python

```python
model = Sequential([
    Embedding(input_dim=10000, output_dim=128),
    LSTM(128, return_sequences=True),
    LSTM(64),
    Dense(32, activation='relu'),
    Dense(1, activation='sigmoid')
])
```

```python
model.compile(optimizer='adam',
loss='binary_crossentropy', metrics=['accuracy'])
```

3. Train and Evaluate the Model

```python
python

# Train model
model.fit(train_data, validation_data=test_data,
epochs=5)

# Evaluate model
loss, accuracy = model.evaluate(test_data)
print(f"Test Accuracy: {accuracy:.4f}")
```

Conclusion

In this chapter, we covered:

✅ Text preprocessing and tokenization
✅ Word embeddings and pre-trained models like Word2Vec and BERT
✅ Recurrent networks (RNNs, LSTMs, GRUs)
✅ Transformers and Attention Mechanisms
✅ Hands-on sentiment analysis project

5. Reinforcement Learning with TensorFlow

Reinforcement Learning (RL) is a machine learning paradigm where an agent learns by interacting with an environment to maximize rewards. TensorFlow provides powerful tools to implement RL algorithms, including Deep Q-Learning and Policy Gradient methods.

In this chapter, we will cover:
✅ Understanding reinforcement learning basics
✅ Deep Q-Learning (DQN) and Policy Gradient methods
✅ Using TensorFlow with OpenAI Gym
✅ Implementing Proximal Policy Optimization (PPO)
✅ Hands-on project: Train an AI to play an Atari game

Understanding Reinforcement Learning Basics

Reinforcement Learning (RL) consists of:

- **Agent**: The AI model making decisions.
- **Environment**: The world where the agent operates (e.g., a game).
- **State**: The current situation of the environment.
- **Action**: The choices the agent can make.
- **Reward**: A score given for taking an action.
- **Policy**: A strategy for selecting actions.

A typical RL loop:
  Observe the environment (state sts_tst).
  Select an action ata_tat based on a policy.
3 ▭▭Receive a reward rtr_trt and observe a new state st+1s_{t+1}st+1.
4 ▭▭Update the policy using reward feedback.
5▭▭ Repeat to improve the agent's performance.

Deep Q-Learning (DQN) and Policy Gradient Methods

Deep Q-Networks (DQN)

DQN is a deep learning-based approach to solving RL problems using a neural network to approximate the **Q-value function**, which helps the agent decide the best action.

Q-function:

$$Q(s,a)=r+\gamma\max Q(s',a')Q(s, a) = r + \gamma \max Q(s', a')Q(s,a)=r+\gamma maxQ(s',a')$$

where γ\gamma$\gamma$ is the discount factor.

Implementing a Deep Q-Network (DQN) in TensorFlow

```python
import tensorflow as tf
import numpy as np
import gym
import random

# Create the environment
```

```python
env = gym.make("CartPole-v1")
state_shape = env.observation_space.shape[0]
action_size = env.action_space.n

# Define Q-network
def create_q_network():
    model = tf.keras.Sequential([
        tf.keras.layers.Dense(24, activation="relu",
input_shape=(state_shape,)),
        tf.keras.layers.Dense(24, activation="relu"),
        tf.keras.layers.Dense(action_size,
activation="linear")
    ])

model.compile(optimizer=tf.keras.optimizers.Adam(lear
ning_rate=0.001), loss="mse")
    return model

q_network = create_q_network()
```

Using TensorFlow with OpenAI Gym

OpenAI Gym provides RL environments for training AI agents.
To interact with Gym:

```python
python

state = env.reset()
done = False

while not done:
    action = env.action_space.sample()  # Select a
random action
    next_state, reward, done, _ = env.step(action)
    env.render()  # Display the environment
env.close()
```

Training an RL Agent with Experience Replay

```python
python

from collections import import deque

memory = deque(maxlen=2000)   # Store past experiences

def train_q_network():
    batch_size = 32
    if len(memory) < batch_size:
        return

    minibatch = random.sample(memory, batch_size)
    for state, action, reward, next_state, done in
minibatch:
        target = reward
        if not done:
            target += 0.95 *
np.amax(q_network.predict(next_state[np.newaxis, :]))

        q_values =
q_network.predict(state[np.newaxis, :])
        q_values[0][action] = target

        q_network.fit(state[np.newaxis, :], q_values,
epochs=1, verbose=0)

# Training loop
for episode in range(1000):
    state = env.reset()
    done = False
    total_reward = 0

    while not done:
        action =
np.argmax(q_network.predict(state[np.newaxis, :]))
        next_state, reward, done, _ =
env.step(action)

        memory.append((state, action, reward,
next_state, done))
        train_q_network()

        state = next_state
        total_reward += reward
```

```
    print(f"Episode {episode}, Total Reward:
{total_reward}")
```

Implementing PPO (Proximal Policy Optimization)

PPO (Proximal Policy Optimization) is a more stable RL algorithm using policy gradients and clipping to optimize the policy safely.

Building a PPO Agent with TensorFlow

```python
python

import tensorflow_probability as tfp

class PPOAgent:
    def __init__(self, state_dim, action_dim,
learning_rate=0.0003):
        self.state_dim = state_dim
        self.action_dim = action_dim

        # Actor network
        self.actor = self.build_actor()
        self.optimizer =
tf.keras.optimizers.Adam(learning_rate)

    def build_actor(self):
        model = tf.keras.Sequential([
            tf.keras.layers.Dense(64,
activation="relu", input_shape=(self.state_dim,)),
            tf.keras.layers.Dense(64,
activation="relu"),
            tf.keras.layers.Dense(self.action_dim,
activation="softmax")
        ])
        return model
```

```python
    def get_action(self, state):
        state = np.expand_dims(state, axis=0)
        probabilities = self.actor(state).numpy()[0]
        return np.random.choice(self.action_dim,
p=probabilities)

# Initialize agent
ppo_agent = PPOAgent(state_dim=state_shape,
action_dim=action_size)

# Get an action
state = env.reset()
action = ppo_agent.get_action(state)
print("Chosen action:", action)
```

Project: Train an AI to Play an Atari Game

Let's train an RL agent to play **Breakout**, a popular Atari game.

1. Install Dependencies

```bash
pip install gym[atari] stable-baselines3
```

2. Use Stable-Baselines3 to Train PPO Agent

```python
from stable_baselines3 import PPO
from stable_baselines3.common.atari_wrappers import
make_atari_env

# Create Atari environment
env = make_atari_env("BreakoutNoFrameskip-v4",
n_envs=1, seed=0)

# Train PPO agent
```

```python
model = PPO("CnnPolicy", env, verbose=1)
model.learn(total_timesteps=100000)

# Save the trained model
model.save("ppo_breakout")
```

3. Play the Game Using the Trained Model

```python
python

# Load trained model
model = PPO.load("ppo_breakout")

obs = env.reset()
done = False
while not done:
    action, _states = model.predict(obs)
    obs, rewards, done, info = env.step(action)
    env.render()
env.close()
```

Conclusion

In this chapter, we covered:

✓ Reinforcement learning fundamentals

✓ Implementing Deep Q-Networks (DQN)

✓ Using TensorFlow with OpenAI Gym

✓ Implementing PPO (Proximal Policy Optimization)

✓ Training an AI to play an Atari game

6. Training & Optimization Techniques

Training deep learning models effectively requires choosing the right optimization algorithms, regularization techniques, and hyperparameter tuning strategies. In this chapter, we'll cover:

✅ Optimizers: Adam, RMSprop, SGD—when to use what
✅ Regularization techniques: Dropout, Batch Normalization
✅ Hyperparameter tuning (Keras Tuner, Bayesian Optimization)
✅ Debugging training issues with TensorBoard

Optimizers: Adam, RMSprop, SGD— When to Use What?

Optimizers determine how a model updates its weights during training. Choosing the right optimizer can significantly impact model performance and training stability.

Optimizer	Best For	Pros	Cons
SGD (Stochastic Gradient Descent)	General-purpose, large datasets	Simple, effective for convex problems	Slow convergence, sensitive to learning rate
RMSprop (Root Mean Square Propagation)	Recurrent Neural Networks (RNNs), NLP	Adaptive learning rate, stable for non-stationary data	Requires fine-tuning of decay rate

| Adam (Adaptive Moment Estimation) | Most deep learning tasks | Fast convergence, adaptive learning rates | Uses more memory |

Implementing Different Optimizers in TensorFlow

```python
import tensorflow as tf

# Define a simple model
model = tf.keras.Sequential([
    tf.keras.layers.Dense(64, activation="relu"),
    tf.keras.layers.Dense(10, activation="softmax")
])

# Try different optimizers
sgd = tf.keras.optimizers.SGD(learning_rate=0.01, momentum=0.9)
adam = tf.keras.optimizers.Adam(learning_rate=0.001)
rmsprop = tf.keras.optimizers.RMSprop(learning_rate=0.001)

# Compile model with Adam optimizer
model.compile(optimizer=adam,
loss="categorical_crossentropy",
metrics=["accuracy"])
```

Regularization Techniques: Dropout, Batch Normalization

Regularization prevents overfitting, ensuring the model generalizes well to unseen data.

Dropout

Dropout randomly deactivates neurons during training to force the model to learn more robust features.

```python
model = tf.keras.Sequential([
    tf.keras.layers.Dense(128, activation="relu"),
    tf.keras.layers.Dropout(0.5),  # 50% neurons
deactivated during training
    tf.keras.layers.Dense(10, activation="softmax")
])
```

Batch Normalization

Batch Normalization normalizes activations within each mini-batch, stabilizing training and speeding up convergence.

```python
model = tf.keras.Sequential([
    tf.keras.layers.Dense(128, activation="relu"),
    tf.keras.layers.BatchNormalization(),
    tf.keras.layers.Dense(10, activation="softmax")
])
```

When to Use?

- **Dropout**: Prevents overfitting, useful for fully connected (dense) layers.
- **Batch Normalization**: Speeds up training, stabilizes deep networks, especially effective for CNNs.

Hyperparameter Tuning: Keras Tuner & Bayesian Optimization

Hyperparameter tuning helps find the best learning rate, batch size, dropout rate, and more.

Using Keras Tuner for Hyperparameter Optimization

```python
python

import keras_tuner as kt

def build_model(hp):
    model = tf.keras.Sequential([
        tf.keras.layers.Dense(hp.Int("units",
min_value=32, max_value=256, step=32),
activation="relu"),

tf.keras.layers.Dropout(hp.Choice("dropout_rate",
[0.2, 0.3, 0.5])),
        tf.keras.layers.Dense(10,
activation="softmax")
    ])
    model.compile(optimizer="adam",
loss="sparse_categorical_crossentropy",
metrics=["accuracy"])
    return model

# Initialize tuner
tuner = kt.RandomSearch(build_model,
objective="val_accuracy", max_trials=5)

# Start search
tuner.search(x_train, y_train, epochs=10,
validation_split=0.2)
best_model = tuner.get_best_models(num_models=1)[0]
```

Bayesian Optimization for Hyperparameter Tuning

Bayesian optimization intelligently selects hyperparameters rather than random search.

```python
from skopt import gp_minimize
from skopt.space import Real, Integer

# Define the search space
space = [Real(1e-5, 1e-1, "log-uniform",
name="learning_rate"),
         Integer(16, 512, name="batch_size")]

# Objective function
def objective(params):
    learning_rate, batch_size = params
    model = tf.keras.models.Sequential([...])  #
Define model

model.compile(optimizer=tf.keras.optimizers.Adam(lear
ning_rate), loss="mse")
    history = model.fit(x_train, y_train,
batch_size=batch_size, epochs=10,
validation_split=0.2)
    return -history.history["val_loss"][-1]

# Optimize hyperparameters
res = gp_minimize(objective, space, n_calls=20)
```

Debugging Training Issues with TensorBoard

TensorBoard is a visualization tool for monitoring model training.

Setting Up TensorBoard

```python
import tensorflow as tf
```

```
import datetime

# Define TensorBoard callback
log_dir = "logs/fit/" +
datetime.datetime.now().strftime("%Y%m%d-%H%M%S")
tensorboard_callback =
tf.keras.callbacks.TensorBoard(log_dir=log_dir,
histogram_freq=1)

# Train model with TensorBoard
model.fit(x_train, y_train, epochs=10,
validation_data=(x_val, y_val),
callbacks=[tensorboard_callback])
```

Launching TensorBoard

Run this in your terminal:

```
bash
```

```
tensorboard --logdir=logs/fit
```

Conclusion

In this chapter, we covered:
✓ Optimizers: When to use Adam, RMSprop, and SGD
✓ Regularization techniques: Dropout & Batch Normalization
✓ Hyperparameter tuning with Keras Tuner & Bayesian Optimization
✓ Debugging training issues with TensorBoard

7. Debugging and Optimization Best Practices

Optimizing TensorFlow models goes beyond selecting the right hyperparameters—it requires efficient memory management, monitoring performance, and leveraging hardware acceleration. This chapter covers:

✅ Monitoring performance with TensorBoard
✅ Memory optimization for large datasets
✅ Using Mixed Precision Training for speedup
✅ Efficient data loading with the `tf.data` pipeline

Monitoring Performance with TensorBoard

TensorBoard is TensorFlow's built-in tool for visualizing model performance, including loss curves, accuracy trends, computational graphs, and system resources.

Setting Up TensorBoard

```python
import tensorflow as tf
import datetime

# Define TensorBoard callback
log_dir = "logs/fit/" + datetime.datetime.now().strftime("%Y%m%d-%H%M%S")
```

```
tensorboard_callback =
tf.keras.callbacks.TensorBoard(log_dir=log_dir,
histogram_freq=1)

# Train model with TensorBoard
model.fit(x_train, y_train, epochs=10,
validation_data=(x_val, y_val),
callbacks=[tensorboard_callback])
```

Launching TensorBoard

Run this command in your terminal:

```
bash
```

```
tensorboard --logdir=logs/fit
```

Key Features of TensorBoard

- **Scalars**: Track training metrics like loss and accuracy
- **Graphs**: Visualize computational graphs for debugging
- **Histograms**: Monitor activation distributions and weights
- **Profiler**: Analyze CPU and GPU utilization

Memory Optimization for Large Datasets

When handling large datasets, inefficient memory usage can lead to slowdowns or crashes. Here's how to optimize memory usage:

1. Enable Garbage Collection

Force TensorFlow to clear unused memory.

```
python
```

```
import gc
```

```
import tensorflow as tf

gc.collect()
tf.keras.backend.clear_session()
```

2. Reduce Model Precision

Switching from `float64` to `float32` or `bfloat16` reduces memory consumption.

python

```
tf.keras.backend.set_floatx('float32')
```

3. Use Gradient Checkpointing

For deep models, TensorFlow's **gradient checkpointing** reduces memory usage.

python

```
from tensorflow.keras.layers import Dense
from tensorflow.keras.models import Model

class CheckpointedModel(Model):
    def call(self, inputs, training=False):
        return tf.recompute_grad(self.model(inputs))

model = CheckpointedModel()
```

4. Free Up GPU Memory

If running multiple experiments, release unused GPU memory.

python

```
from numba import cuda
cuda.select_device(0)
cuda.close()
```

Using Mixed Precision Training for Speedup

Mixed precision uses lower precision (e.g., **float16**) for faster training while maintaining accuracy.

Enable Mixed Precision in TensorFlow

```python
python

import tensorflow as tf
from tensorflow.keras.mixed_precision import
experimental as mixed_precision

# Enable mixed precision
policy = mixed_precision.Policy('mixed_float16')
mixed_precision.set_policy(policy)
```

Why Use Mixed Precision?

✅ **Faster Training**: Uses Tensor Cores on modern GPUs (NVIDIA Ampere & later)
✅ **Less Memory Usage**: Reduces weight and activation sizes
✅ **Minimal Accuracy Loss**: Keeps important calculations in `float32`

Efficient Data Loading with `tf.data` Pipeline

Using the `tf.data` API, you can efficiently load and preprocess large datasets in parallel.

1. Load a Dataset Efficiently

```python
import tensorflow as tf

def preprocess(image, label):
    image = tf.image.resize(image, (128, 128)) / 255.0
    return image, label

batch_size = 32
AUTOTUNE = tf.data.AUTOTUNE  # Automatically optimize performance

dataset = tf.keras.datasets.cifar10.load_data()
(x_train, y_train), (x_test, y_test) = dataset

train_ds = (tf.data.Dataset.from_tensor_slices((x_train, y_train))
            .map(preprocess, num_parallel_calls=AUTOTUNE)
            .shuffle(10000)
            .batch(batch_size)
            .prefetch(AUTOTUNE))  # Prefetch improves performance
```

2. Use TFRecord Format for Faster Loading

TFRecord is a binary format that speeds up data reading.

Convert Data to TFRecord

```python
import tensorflow as tf

def serialize_example(image, label):
    feature = {
```

```python
        "image":
tf.train.Feature(bytes_list=tf.train.BytesList(value=
[image.numpy().tobytes()])),
        "label":
tf.train.Feature(int64_list=tf.train.Int64List(value=
[label.numpy()]))
    }
    example =
tf.train.Example(features=tf.train.Features(feature=f
eature))
    return example.SerializeToString()

with tf.io.TFRecordWriter("train.tfrecord") as
writer:
    for image, label in zip(x_train, y_train):
        writer.write(serialize_example(image, label))
```

Load TFRecord Dataset

```python
def parse_tfrecord(example_proto):
    features = {
        "image": tf.io.FixedLenFeature([],
tf.string),
        "label": tf.io.FixedLenFeature([], tf.int64)
    }
    parsed_features =
tf.io.parse_single_example(example_proto, features)
    image =
tf.io.decode_raw(parsed_features["image"], tf.uint8)
    image = tf.reshape(image, [32, 32, 3])  # Reshape
based on dataset
    return image, parsed_features["label"]

dataset =
tf.data.TFRecordDataset("train.tfrecord").map(parse_t
frecord).batch(32)
```

Conclusion

In this chapter, we covered:

✓ **Monitoring performance with TensorBoard** for visualization

✓ **Memory optimization techniques** to handle large datasets

✓ **Mixed Precision Training** for faster execution

✓ **Efficient data loading** with the `tf.data` pipeline and TFRecords

8. Model Deployment & Production

Deploying a trained TensorFlow model is the final step in making your AI solution accessible. This chapter covers:

✅ Saving and loading TensorFlow models
✅ Deploying models with **TensorFlow Serving** and **TensorFlow Lite**
✅ Running models on **Google Cloud AI, AWS, and Colab**
✅ Deploying models on **mobile and edge devices**

Saving and Loading TensorFlow Models

After training a model, saving it ensures you can reuse it later without retraining.

Saving a Model

There are two main formats:
   SavedModel format (recommended for deployment)
   HDF5 format (.h5, common for Keras models)

Save as a SavedModel format

```python

model.save("saved_model/my_model")  # Saves
architecture, weights, and optimizer state
```

Save as a .h5 file

```python

model.save("my_model.h5")
```

Loading a Saved Model

```python
python

new_model =
tf.keras.models.load_model("saved_model/my_model")
```

Deploying Models with TensorFlow Serving

TensorFlow Serving is a system designed for serving ML models in production.

1. Install TensorFlow Serving

```bash
bash

pip install tensorflow-serving-api
```

2. Export the Model for Serving

```python
python

model.save("serving_model/1")   # The folder structure
must contain version numbers
```

3. Start TensorFlow Serving

```bash
bash

tensorflow_model_server --rest_api_port=8501 --
model_base_path="$(pwd)/serving_model"
```

4. Make a Prediction Using REST API

```bash
bash

curl -d '{"signature_name":"serving_default",
"instances":[[1.0, 2.0, 3.0]]}' \
```

49

```
    -H "Content-Type: application/json" \
    -X POST
http://localhost:8501/v1/models/my_model:predict
```

Deploying with TensorFlow Lite (TFLite) for Mobile & Edge Devices

TensorFlow Lite (TFLite) allows you to deploy models on **mobile (Android, iOS) and edge devices (Raspberry Pi, IoT)**.

1. Convert a Model to TensorFlow Lite

python

```python
converter =
tf.lite.TFLiteConverter.from_saved_model("saved_model
/my_model")
tflite_model = converter.convert()

# Save the converted model
with open("model.tflite", "wb") as f:
    f.write(tflite_model)
```

2. Load and Run Inference on TFLite

python

```python
import tensorflow.lite as tflite
import numpy as np

interpreter =
tflite.Interpreter(model_path="model.tflite")
interpreter.allocate_tensors()

input_details = interpreter.get_input_details()
output_details = interpreter.get_output_details()

# Example input
```

```
input_data = np.array([[1.0, 2.0, 3.0]],
dtype=np.float32)
interpreter.set_tensor(input_details[0]['index'],
input_data)

# Run inference
interpreter.invoke()
output_data =
interpreter.get_tensor(output_details[0]['index'])
print(output_data)
```

3. Deploy TFLite Model on Android

- Use **TensorFlow Lite Interpreter API** in Android Studio
- Optimize model size using **TensorFlow Model Optimization Toolkit**

Deploying Models on Cloud Platforms

1. Google Cloud AI Platform

Google Cloud AI allows you to deploy TensorFlow models at scale.

Upload and Deploy a Model

bash

```
gcloud ai models create my_model --region=us-central1
gcloud ai versions create v1 --model=my_model --
origin=gs://my-bucket/saved_model/
```

Run Prediction on Google Cloud

python

```
from google.cloud import aiplatform
client = aiplatform.gapic.PredictionServiceClient()

response =
client.predict(endpoint="my_model_endpoint",
instances=[[1.0, 2.0, 3.0]])
print(response)
```

2. Deploying on AWS (SageMaker)

AWS SageMaker provides an easy way to deploy TensorFlow
models.

Upload Model to S3

bash

```
aws s3 cp saved_model/my_model s3://my-
bucket/tensorflow-model/
```

Deploy Model Using SageMaker

python

```
import sagemaker
from sagemaker.tensorflow import TensorFlowModel

sagemaker_model =
TensorFlowModel(model_data="s3://my-
bucket/tensorflow-model",

role="SageMakerRole",

framework_version="2.8")

predictor =
sagemaker_model.deploy(instance_type="ml.m5.large")
```

3. Running on Google Colab

You can deploy a model in Google Colab using **FastAPI**.

```python
python

from fastapi import FastAPI
import tensorflow as tf
import uvicorn

app = FastAPI()
model =
tf.keras.models.load_model("saved_model/my_model")

@app.post("/predict/")
def predict(data: dict):
    input_data = np.array(data["instances"])
    predictions = model.predict(input_data)
    return {"predictions": predictions.tolist()}

if __name__ == "__main__":
    uvicorn.run(app, host="0.0.0.0", port=5000)
```

Run the app:

```bash
bash

uvicorn my_api:app --host 0.0.0.0 --port 5000
```

Deploying Models on Mobile and Edge Devices

✅ **Android & iOS:** Use **TFLite Interpreter** for running models on mobile.
✅ **Raspberry Pi & IoT:** Use **TFLite + Edge TPU** for optimized inference.

✅ **Web Deployment:** Convert models to **TensorFlow.js** for browser-based inference.

Convert Model for TensorFlow.js

python

```
!pip install tensorflowjs
!tensorflowjs_converter --input_format=tf_saved_model
saved_model/my_model tfjs_model/
```

Load in JavaScript:

javascript

```
const model = await
tf.loadLayersModel('tfjs_model/model.json');
const prediction = model.predict(tf.tensor([1.0, 2.0,
3.0]));
```

Conclusion

In this chapter, we covered:
✅ **Saving and loading models** for reuse
✅ **TensorFlow Serving** for API-based deployment
✅ **TensorFlow Lite (TFLite)** for mobile and edge deployment
✅ **Cloud deployment** on **Google Cloud AI, AWS SageMaker, and Colab**
✅ **Deploying models in JavaScript with TensorFlow.js**

9. Real-World Projects & Case Studies

This chapter covers **hands-on projects** that apply TensorFlow to real-world problems in **Computer Vision, Natural Language Processing (NLP), and Reinforcement Learning (RL).**

Each project follows a **step-by-step** approach, with **dataset selection, model design, training, and deployment.**

---

1. Computer Vision: Image Segmentation with U-Net

What is Image Segmentation?

Unlike classification, **image segmentation** divides an image into multiple regions (objects, backgrounds, etc.). It's widely used in **medical imaging, autonomous driving, and satellite imagery**.

Dataset: The Oxford-IIIT Pet Dataset

The dataset contains images of **cats and dogs** with segmentation masks.

Step 1: Load and Preprocess the Dataset

```python
import tensorflow as tf
import tensorflow_datasets as tfds
```

```python
dataset, info = tfds.load('oxford_iiit_pet',
with_info=True, as_supervised=True)
```

Step 2: Define the U-Net Model

python

```python
from tensorflow.keras import layers, Model

def unet_model():
    inputs = layers.Input(shape=(128, 128, 3))
    x = layers.Conv2D(64, (3, 3), activation='relu',
padding='same')(inputs)
    x = layers.MaxPooling2D((2, 2))(x)
    x = layers.Conv2D(128, (3, 3), activation='relu',
padding='same')(x)
    x = layers.UpSampling2D((2, 2))(x)
    outputs = layers.Conv2D(1, (1, 1),
activation='sigmoid', padding='same')(x)

    return Model(inputs, outputs)

model = unet_model()
model.compile(optimizer="adam",
loss="binary_crossentropy", metrics=["accuracy"])
```

Step 3: Train the Model

python

```python
model.fit(train_data, epochs=20,
validation_data=val_data)
```

Step 4: Evaluate & Visualize

python

```python
import matplotlib.pyplot as plt

sample_image = next(iter(test_data))[0].numpy()
predicted_mask =
model.predict(sample_image.reshape(1, 128, 128, 3))
```

```
plt.subplot(1, 2, 1)
plt.imshow(sample_image)
plt.subplot(1, 2, 2)
plt.imshow(predicted_mask.squeeze(), cmap="gray")
plt.show()
```

✅ **End Result:** The trained U-Net model can segment images by identifying objects like cats and dogs.

---

2. NLP: Text Summarization with Transformers

What is Text Summarization?

Text summarization extracts the most important information from long documents. There are **two types:**

- **Extractive summarization:** Picks key sentences.
- **Abstractive summarization:** Generates new sentences.

We'll build an **abstractive summarization model** using **Hugging Face Transformers + TensorFlow.**

Dataset: CNN/Daily Mail News Articles

python

```
from datasets import load_dataset

dataset = load_dataset("cnn_dailymail", "3.0.0")
```

Step 1: Load a Pretrained Transformer Model

python

```python
from transformers import TFAutoModelForSeq2SeqLM,
AutoTokenizer

tokenizer = AutoTokenizer.from_pretrained("t5-small")
model = TFAutoModelForSeq2SeqLM.from_pretrained("t5-
small")
```

Step 2: Preprocess the Text

python

```python
def preprocess_function(examples):
    inputs = ["summarize: " + doc for doc in
examples["article"]]
    model_inputs = tokenizer(inputs, max_length=512,
truncation=True, padding="max_length",
return_tensors="tf")
    return model_inputs

dataset = dataset.map(preprocess_function,
batched=True)
```

Step 3: Fine-Tune the Model

python

```python
model.compile(optimizer="adam",
loss=model.compute_loss, metrics=["accuracy"])
model.fit(dataset["train"], epochs=3)
```

Step 4: Generate Summaries

python

```python
input_text = "summarize: " + "AI is transforming the
world by automating complex tasks..."
input_ids = tokenizer.encode(input_text,
return_tensors="tf")
output = model.generate(input_ids)
print(tokenizer.decode(output[0],
skip_special_tokens=True))
```

✅ **End Result:** The model generates concise summaries of long news articles.

---

3. Reinforcement Learning: AI-Powered Game Bot with Deep RL

What is Deep Reinforcement Learning?

RL trains an **agent** to maximize rewards in an environment. This project uses **Deep Q-Learning (DQN)** to train an AI to play **Atari Breakout**.

Step 1: Setup the Gym Environment

python

```
import gym
import numpy as np

env = gym.make("Breakout-v0")
state = env.reset()
```

Step 2: Define the DQN Model

python

```
from tensorflow.keras.models import Sequential
from tensorflow.keras.layers import Dense, Conv2D,
Flatten

def build_dqn():
    model = Sequential([
        Conv2D(32, (8, 8), strides=(4, 4),
activation="relu", input_shape=(84, 84, 4)),
        Conv2D(64, (4, 4), strides=(2, 2),
activation="relu"),
```

```
        Flatten(),
        Dense(512, activation="relu"),
        Dense(env.action_space.n,
activation="linear")
    ])
    return model

dqn_model = build_dqn()
```

Step 3: Train the AI

```python
import random

def train_dqn(episodes=500):
    for episode in range(episodes):
        state = env.reset()
        total_reward = 0

        while True:
            action = env.action_space.sample()   #
Random action
            next_state, reward, done, _ =
env.step(action)
            total_reward += reward
            if done:
                break
        print(f"Episode {episode+1}: Total Reward:
{total_reward}")

train_dqn()
```

Step 4: Play the Game with the Trained Model

```python
state = env.reset()
done = False

while not done:
```

```
    action =
np.argmax(dqn_model.predict(state.reshape(1, 84, 84,
4)))
    state, reward, done, _ = env.step(action)
    env.render()
```

✅ **End Result:** The AI learns to **play Breakout**, improving over time.

Conclusion

In this chapter, we explored **three real-world AI projects**:
✓ **Computer Vision:** Image segmentation with U-Net
✓ **NLP:** Summarization using Transformers
✓ **Reinforcement Learning:** AI game bot with Deep Q-Learning

These projects provide **practical experience** in **building, training, and deploying AI models**.

10. Conclusion & Next Steps

Congratulations on reaching the end of this guide! You've gained a solid foundation in **TensorFlow**, covering everything from **basic operations** to **deep learning, computer vision, NLP, reinforcement learning, and deployment**.

But the journey doesn't end here! AI and machine learning are **fast-evolving fields**, and staying updated is key to mastering TensorFlow.

---

1. Recommended Resources for Further Learning

To continue expanding your knowledge, here are some top resources:

Books & Official Documentation

- <u>TensorFlow Documentation</u> – The best place to explore new features and APIs.
- **Deep Learning with Python** by François Chollet – A fantastic deep dive into **Keras** and deep learning.
- **Hands-On Machine Learning with Scikit-Learn, Keras, and TensorFlow** by Aurélien Géron – Covers **practical ML workflows**.

Online Courses & Tutorials

- <u>TensorFlow Developer Certificate Course (Coursera)</u>
- <u>Fast.ai Deep Learning Course</u> – Practical deep learning techniques.

- **Stanford CS231n: Convolutional Neural Networks** – A deep dive into **computer vision**.

Open-Source TensorFlow Projects to Explore

- **TensorFlow Hub** (tfhub.dev) – Pre-trained models for transfer learning.
- **DeepMind's RL Baselines** (GitHub) – Reinforcement learning research.
- **Hugging Face Transformers** (GitHub) – NLP models for text generation, classification, and more.

2. Joining the TensorFlow Community

Being part of a community helps you stay motivated and updated. Here's where to connect with TensorFlow experts:

TensorFlow Forums & GitHub

- **TensorFlow Discuss Forum** – Ask and answer technical questions.
- **TensorFlow GitHub** – Contribute to TensorFlow's open-source projects.

Engage on Social Media & Meetups

- **Follow TensorFlow on Twitter/X**: @TensorFlow
- **Join AI Slack & Discord Communities**
- **Attend AI Conferences**: NeurIPS, CVPR, ICML

3. Future Trends in AI & TensorFlow

The field of AI is advancing rapidly. Here are some key trends to watch:

1. Generative AI & Large Language Models (LLMs)

- Models like **ChatGPT, Gemini, and Llama** are evolving quickly.
- TensorFlow is integrating with **Transformers, Stable Diffusion**, and generative AI.

2. AI on Edge & Mobile Devices

- TensorFlow Lite enables **faster, more efficient AI on smartphones, IoT, and embedded devices**.
- Google is optimizing AI chips (TPUs) for real-time inference.

3. Multimodal AI (Vision + NLP + Speech)

- **Vision Transformers (ViTs), Audio Transformers**, and **Multimodal AI** are gaining traction.
- TensorFlow is supporting more **cross-domain AI research**.

4. AI for Sustainability & Ethical AI

- AI models are being designed for **energy efficiency and carbon reduction**.
- Ethical AI practices (bias detection, fairness) are becoming a key focus.

Final Words: Keep Experimenting & Building!

AI is a **continuous learning process**. The best way to master TensorFlow is to **experiment, work on projects, and collaborate with the community**.

Whether you're **building an AI startup, training models for research, or just having fun experimenting**, the possibilities with TensorFlow are endless.

 Next Step: Start your own **TensorFlow project** and share it with the world!

Table of Contents :

www.ingramcontent.com/pod-product-compliance
Lightning Source LLC
LaVergne TN
LVHW052129070326

832902LV00039B/4519